Irish Gentleman

Defence of opposition with respect to their conduct on Irish affairs

With explanatory notes dedicated to the Right Honourable C.J. Fox

Irish Gentleman

Defence of opposition with respect to their conduct on Irish affairs
With explanatory notes dedicated to the Right Honourable C.J. Fox

ISBN/EAN: 9783337196592

Printed in Europe, USA, Canada, Australia, Japan

Cover: Foto ©ninafisch / pixelio.de

More available books at **www.hansebooks.com**

DEFENCE of OPPOSITION

WITH RESPECT TO

THEIR CONDUCT

ON

IRISH AFFAIRS,

WITH

EXPLANATORY NOTES.

DEDICATED

TO THE RIGHT HONOURABLE

C. J. FOX.

BY AN IRISH GENTLEMAN,

A MEMBER OF THE WHIG CLUB.

DUBLIN:

PRINTED FOR L. WHITE, No. 86, DAME-STREET;
AND P. BYRNE, No. 35, COLLEGE-GREEN.

M,DCC,LXXXV.

TO THE

RIGHT HON. J. C. FOX.

SIR,

THE founding a commercial intercourse between Great Britain and Ireland, upon the basis of mutual advantage, seems a measure so wise, and salutary in itself, and so promising in its confequences, as naturally to excite a more than ordinary share of the public attention.

The object has long had the warmest wishes of the best, and most exalted characters of both countries, and the most fervent prayers of every one not insensible of their welfare and happiness; and it is with inexpreffible pleasure and satisfaction, they now behold it ripening, and nearly brought to a state of maturity, by the fostering hand of the present most excellent Minister, who, with his father's resplendent virtues, most happily blends the wisdom of age and experience.

A Measure, Sir, that will at once do away all those jealoufies that have fo long filled the breast of Ireland—that must for ever attach her to Great Britain—and make their interest one and the same, cannot but claim a very powerful support from the representatives of the people.

It

It is, therefore, with much furprize, the public hear, that you, and thofe you are in the habit of voting with, (including your *new* friends) intend to give it every oppofition in your power.

The *confiftency* of your conduct, in the line of politics, gives, at once, the flatteft contradiction to fo impudent and barefaced a calumny.

The following fheets, however, will effectually put the matter out of doubt, and do you ample juftice.

They are the faithful extracts of various fpeeches delivered in Parliament by *you*, and *thofe* you have the honour to act with, and will be found to contain the ftrongeft recommendations of the *very* meafures, now under difcuffion, for eftablifhing a fair and equal trade between Great Britain and Ireland.

You will pleafe, therefore, to accept of them as the beft, and moft conclufive refutation of the charges brought againft you, as from them, it is impoffible, confidering how very unlikely *you* are to be actuated by party views, that the minifter can want *your* fupport and affiftance.

I have the honor to be,

CONTENTS.

CONTENTS.

A P P E N D I X.

The COMMERCIAL RESOLUTIONS of the IRISH PARLIA-
MENT in their preſent Seſſion VINDICATED.   Page 4!

HOUSE of COMMONS.

Mr. SAWBRIDGE.

I Am againſt all monopolies of trade, and commercial interdictions; there is trade enough for every nation upon earth, *if all impolitic reſtrictions were repealed.* No nation, nor corporate body, nor individual, has a right to deprive another *of the benefits of manufactures, trade, and commerce.*

March 18, 1779*.

Mr. BURKE.

It is for the *intereſt* of Great Britain to throw open *even the woollen trade to Ireland;* and if it is not done now voluntarily, the French will foon oblige us to do it.

March 18, 1779.

B   Lord

The order of the day was for going into a committee on the importation of fugars into Ireland, which was loſt on a diviſion, 62 to 58.

Lord BEAUCHAMP.

The language the noble Lord, (Earl of Hilſbo-rough) uſed in the other Houſe of the late miniſ-ters, (Lord North, &c.) clearly meant an equality of export and import duties, cuſtoms, &c. an equa-lity of trade, and conſequently of mutual advan-tage.   *Nov.* 30, 1779.

Earl of UPPER OSSORY.

As an Iriſhman, and bound to Ireland by the ſtrongeſt ties of intereſt and affection, it might be fairly, and I will add, be truly preſumed, that I entertain the moſt ſincere wiſhes for her happineſs and proſperity; nay, I will ſay, that as an Eng-liſhman, it is my duty to do ſo, becauſe I am per-ſuaded, *that whatever promotes the trade and com-merce of* Ireland, *will ultimately promote that of* Great Britain.   *Dec.* 6, 1779.

Lord BEAUCHAMP.

That Ireland is in a diſtreſſed ſituation, no man within or without this Houſe will, I dare ſay, venture to deny; but I can never be perſuaded to think, that the miſeries which Ireland feels, and under which ſhe at preſent groans, can be fairly attributed to the preſent miniſtry, or indeed to any miniſtry within my remembrance. The grievance has

has not originated, at leaft fince the prefent reign, with any particular fet of men in power, nor from any recent meafures adopted in refpect to that country. The caufes are various, *but the prime fource* of the diftreffes of that kingdom, *is the fyftem of our trade laws*, which lay *a reftraint upon her commerce*. I am convinced, that thefe reftrictions arife from a very narrow, fhort-fighted policy, conceived in prejudice, and ftrengthened by time; which, after more than a century, has been wrought, as it were, into the very conftitution of this country.

For my own part, I think *the intereft of both countries is infeparable*, as their political connexion is indiffoluble, and whoever endeavours to obftruct either, *is no friend to his country*, that is, *he is ignorant of the true profperity of both*.

Though enjoying a place under the Crown, my fituation is not fuch, as to entitle me to know what paffes in his Majefty's council; but I have heard in converfation, that the noble Lord on the fame bench, (Lord *North*) in concert with the reft of his Majefty's fervants, have agreed upon propofitions,

B 2

* As neither Lord *North*, Mr. *Fox*, nor Mr. *Burke*, can be thought *ignorant* of the true profperity of both England and Ireland, according to Lord *Beauchamp*, neither of them *is a friend to his country*; and they will hardly have the ill manners to contradict a noble Lord they fo cordially act with.

pofitions, which are to be fubmitted to this houfe. I am ignorant of their purport; but from what I heard fall from a noble Lord (Earl of Hilfborough) in the other houfe, the firft day of the feffion; to whom, both England, and Ireland, owe the higheft obligations, it is fuppofed, *that Ireland will be granted an equal trade, or an equality of trade,* upon the broad bafis, of impartiality and juftice.

Dec. 6, 1779.

Mr. BURKE.

Ireland fpurns at the Britifh claim of dominion: fhe looks upon herfelf as *free and independent,* and is firmly determined to maintain it. The American war originated in injuftice, has been conducted with cruelty, and is likely to end in infamy, difgrace, and difappointment. The loyalty of the people of Ireland can no more procure juftice at the hands of minifters, than the ftubborn fpirit of America. Ireland, driven to the laft ftage of human mifery and diftrefs, is left to her wretched fate; fhe intreats—fhe fupplicates—but in vain. Without a pretence of offence on her part, fhe is left to fate, unattended to, and unpitied!

Ireland now will not be fatisfied *with any thing fhort of a free trade.* The people of Ireland have reafoned fairly and juftly: the colonies, they know, have been offered the moft that their own

moft

moſt ſanguine expectations could aſpire to, a free trade with all the world. America, for her revolt, has had a choice of favours held out to her: This is the reward of rebellion, Ireland for her loyalty, for almoſt a century, and her forbearance under accumulated oppreſſion, and internal diſtreſſes, has been refuſed the mighty indulgence of importing her own ſugars; at all events, without taking any peculiar merit with the Britiſh Government, for their loyal, faithful, and peaceable demeanor, they thought they were at leaſt entitled to meet the colonies upon equal terms, and with equal expectations of favour and relief to thoſe which America has ſpurned at with contempt.

I am induced, from every conſideration, which ſtrikes me, to believe, *that whatever meaſure will ſerve Ireland eſſentially, will, and muſt, in the end, ſerve England.* Dec. 6, 1779.

Mr. FOX.

It is the general calamities of the empire, that has made Ireland *poor*; but it is the incapacity and negligence of government, that has rendered her bold and daring. It is therefore incumbent upon parliament, to ſhew their fulleſt diſapprobation of that indolence and incapacity; and convince Ireland, that they.are as ready as themſelves to reſent and puniſh the cruel and improper treatment,

ment, which they have received from minifters. Ireland will fee by fuch a conduct, that it is not this country, but its minifters who are blameable, which will, in my opinion, prove the fureft means of once more binding both countries in the ftrongeft, and moft indiffoluble ties of friendfhip and affection.   *Dec.* 6, 1779.

Lord N O R T H.

Many favours have been granted to Ireland, fince I have had the honour of a feat in his Majefty's councils, fuch as the free importation of beef and butter rendered perpetual; the encouragement given to the Newfoundland cod fifhery; and the Southern whale fifhery, by bounties granted by the Britifh parliament; the giving leave to export woollen for clothing the troops on the Irifh eftablifhment, ferving out of that kingdom; the act for encouraging the culture of tobacco and hemp, by permitting its importation into Great Britain; the permiffion of the export of feveral enumerated articles to the Britifh fugar colonies, and the coaft of Africa, &c. Thefe favours, howfoever liberally given, have not anfwered, nor proved fufficiently efficacious in removing the difficulties the people of Ireland labour under, *from the reftrictions laid upon her trade,* nor *the diftreffes that are the confequences of thofe reftrictions.* What parliament may
do,

do, is not for me to foretell, nor dictate; but I pre-
fume, they will come with the beſt diſpoſitions
towards their brethren in Ireland, *and grant them
every thing which does not apparently claſh with the eſſential intereſts of this kingdom.*   *Dec.* 6, 1779.

Mr. WELBORE ELLIS,

Though a native of Ireland, I riſe as a member
of this houſe, to give my opinion, relative to the
intereſt of my conſtituents, and am happy to find
myſelf in a ſituation, when I can unite a ſtrict diſ-
charge of my duty with my native feelings. *The
intereſts* of Great Britain and Ireland *are reciprocal
and mutual.*   *Dec.* 6, 1779.

Lord GEO. GERMAINE.

Perſons of great weight and ability in this kingdom have been conſulted on the ſubject of our
differences with Ireland, but their opinions were
ſo contradictory, that no certain information, or
what would promiſe to give ſatisfaction, could be
obtained, ſufficient to ground meaſures upon, and
conſequently neither Miniſtry, nor Parliament
could decide, *till a proper ſpecification was made by
the People of Ireland,* through the only channel on
which it could be relied on, or attended to. That
ſpecification has been made; the Iriſh Parliament
have come to an unanimous vote, *that nothing ſhort*

of

of a free trade would anſwer the object which their preſent ſituation neceſſarily points to. The Iriſh Parliament has been explicit, *and I hope that their deſires will be granted* *.   *Dec.* 6, 1779.

Lord NORTH.

I mean now to open my three propoſitions, relative to the allowing Ireland a free export of her wool, woollens, and wool flocks ; a free exportation of glaſs, and of all kinds of glaſs manufactures ; of a freedom of trade with the Britiſh plantations ; on certain conditions, the baſis of which is to be *an equality of taxes and cuſtoms, upon an equal and unreſtrained trade.*

To demonſtrate the matter of right, as well as favour, I beg leave to ſtate the two following propoſitions : Firſt, *That Ireland has a free and unlimited right to trade with the whole world.* Secondly, That Ireland does not, nor cannot, pretend to claim any right, directly, or co-relatively, with any part of the Britiſh colonies, or plantations. Every perſon in both kingdoms, muſt inſtantly give an univerſal aſſent to the latter propoſition. It is not my wiſh to enter into a diſcuſſion of the former, or debate points merely ſpeculatively : ſo much,

---

* Nothing can poſſibly be more agreeable to this, than the conduct obſerved by the preſent miniſter towards Ireland.

much, however, I will hazard, that mixing the broad claim of a free and unreftrained trade, and qualifying it with the advantage derivable from a connection with Great-Britain, it will not be too much to fay, that although the claim is with Ireland, the option of a connexion with this country, and a participation of commercial intereft, *is clearly in favor of Great-Britain.*

It is both the intereft, and inclination of Ireland, to ftand well with England, and on the idea of fuch a natural and political connexion ; they have been rather harfhly and impolitically treated : *before the Reftoration they enjoyed every commercial advantage and benefit in common with England.*

The commerce, import and export, was held in common by both kingdoms till the reign of Charles the Second: even the act of navigation, the great foundation of our plantation laws, put England and Ireland upon exact terms of equality ; nor was it till two years after that the firft commercial reftriction was laid on Ireland, and that not directly, but by a fide wind, and by deductive interpretation. When the act firft paffed, there was a general governing claufe, for giving bonds to perform the conditions of the act, but then the act was amended, in the fifteenth of Charles the Second : whence a conclufion was drawn, that the acts of the two preceding Parliaments, twelfth,

C   thirteenth,

thirteenth, and fourteenth of Charles the Second, were thereby repealed, though it was as clearly expreffed in thefe acts, as it was poffible for words to convey, that fhips built in Ireland, *navigated with the people thereof*, were deemed Britifh, and qualified to trade to and from the Britifh plantations; and that fhips built in Ireland, and navigated with his Majefty's fubjects of Ireland, *were entitled to the fame abatements and privileges, to which importers and exporters of goods in Britifh built fhips were entitled by the book of rates.*

Upon an average of the fix years, from 1766 to 1772, the export to Ireland was fomething more than two millions; and in the fucceeding fix years, ending in 1778, about as much more, one half nearly Britifh manufacture or produce, the other half certificated articles, of which this country was the medium of conveyance; out of the native produce, which was fomething more than 900,000l. per annum, on the average, only 200,000 were woollens; fo that in this light, fuppofing every thing that any man could wifh to conclude from the fact, I muft fubmit to the Houfe, whether it would be found policy to rifque *a million export* of native produce, for a woollen export of 200,000l.

The woollen manufacture muft, indeed, a long time continue in a ftate of infancy; and though cloths have been manufactured fufficient to anfwer

a con-a confiderable part of the home confumption, yet it can hardly be expected that Ireland will be able to rival Great Britain at the foreign markets, when, after the expence of land carriage, freight, infurance, factorage, &c. fhe is able to underfell Ireland in her own markets on the very fpot, though aided by the advantage of low wages and taxes.

Should the Irifh be permitted to enjoy a free export of woollens, I fhould ftill be for continuing the bounties paid on the exportation from England of certain fpecies of fabrics of Irifh Linens.

The fubject demands much confideration, and requires much modelling. It is a matter of infinite delicacy, and will call for a great deal of detail and enquiry, and therefore ought not to be hurried on.

Though under different legiflatures, Great-Britain and Ireland *have but one conjugal intereft*; and are, in the general fenfe of the phrafe, BUT ONE PEOPLE. Even fhould fhe (Ireland) be enabled to rival us in foreign markets, in a few commodities of native growth, cheapnefs of labour, and other incidental circumftances, we fhould not forget *that Ireland forms a part of the Britifh Empire.*

Dec. 13, 1719.

Lord

Lord N O R T H.

In one article of Importation, viz. *that of sugar*, Ireland may probably ſtill chooſe to take them *circuitouſly* through England, at the low duties, in preference to *directly* importing them at the high duties.   *Jan.* 24, 1780.

Mr. E D E N.

Will it not be expedient to anticipate the wiſhes of Ireland, and convince her of our ſincere intentions, to give her every ſecurity in our power for the permanency of her conſtitution, and of that trade which ſhe is ſo anxious to preſerve ? *

April 18, 1782.

Mr. F O X †.

The diſpoſition of the King's miniſters towards Ireland, I believe, is ſufficiently underſtood; and that diſpoſition, which they have expreſſed, *when*
out

---

* On the 2d of February, 1785, the following Reſolutions were *unanimouſly* agreed to, viz. to allow the exporting, carrying or conveying *corn* out of this realm into Ireland ; to admit *foreign hops* there ; and to repeal the acts which take off *the drawbacks on Britiſh hops*; and for the Iriſh to be admitted to *the Turkey Company*, &c.   No oppoſition was given to theſe Reſolutions, nor any debate had thereon.

† At this time one of his Majeſty's principal Secretaries of State.

out of office, I sincerely believe they will now maintain, and will take the speediest and most likely
means of giving *compleat satisfaction to the people of
Ireland.*

I trust in the candor of the House, for the confidence which they will have in the intentions of his
Majesty's Ministers towards Ireland; and that
they will believe that they mean and wish most
ardently to bring the matter forward in the most
speedy manner. I will again assure them that
it has always been my political sentiment, that
it is unjust and tyrannical to attempt to hold a
country in subjection, and to govern against the
will and opinion of the people. It has always been
my sentiments with regard to America, as well as
Ireland, that they cannot, much less ought not to
be governed by laws which they reject as uncon-
stitutional. All just Government must consist in
the perfect consent, good will, and opinion of the
people; it is the best and surest system of Government where harmony prevails; and without it,
it is not Government, but *usurpation.*

It is certainly the most consistent with true policy, as well as justice, to bring about a final settlement of the dispute between Great-Britain and
Ireland; to state, and precisely to declare, *not
for a moment,* but for ever, what is the relative
situation of the two countries with respect to each
other;

other ; to take in and conclude all the points of difference, and to eftablifh fuch a *fyftem* of connexion, intimacy, and relation between them, as fhall be immediately, and permanently, for the intereft of both. To be fettled for ages, and not, as has been the conduct of late minifters, fear up the wound for a moment, without compleating the cure. When thofe minifters agreed to the extenfion of the trade with Ireland, they fhould have ultimately fettled the claim, and fixed the fituation. They failed to do this at the proper time, and they ought to anfwer for it to their country; *that meafures however will be ufed for accomplifhing this defirable end, I may fafely affure the houfe.** I think that deceit is always pernicious, and I wifh to fpeak with as much opennefs, and information, as the nature of my office can juftify.

April 8, 1782.

Mr. SHERIDAN.

The attack made by the Honourable Gentleman (Mr. Eden) on the new minifters, is fcandaloufly unfair, *as I am convinced that they* † *have the faireft intentions towards Ireland.* *April* 8, 1782.

Mr.

* What *but this*, is Mr. *Fox*, and his party, *now* oppofing in the Houfe of Commons ?—

† Meaning, no doubt, Lord *North*, Mr. *Fox*, &c.

Mr. F O X.

His Majesty is most earnestly desirous of settling the discontents and jealousies that subsist in the minds of his subjects of the kingdom of Ireland. The measures which his Majesty's ministers conceive necessary to be taken in the present instance, and which I am to propose to the House, *will require a great deal of most serious discussion.* The House will perceive, that in the pretensions of the Irish, expressed by the parliament and people, that the matter contains no less than the constitution of the kingdom, that it comprehends not only the commercial rights, and privileges of the kingdom, but also the legislative power and royalty. The most important objects are therefore embraced, and both nations are most materially concerned, in the discussion and settlement of the matter: they are topics, upon which they will see his Majesty cannot decide, without the assistance of his parliament; nor *indeed without the assistance and concurrence of both parliaments.* To come to the business therefore with property, and in a manner that will give effect to their proceedings, they must have full and authentic information; *and both parliaments must take time in their deliberation.** *April* 4, 1782.

Hon.

* Every possible information has been sought after by the *present minister,* and time given *for the fullest deliberation* on the subject of Irish affairs.

Hon. Colonel F I T Z P A T R I C K.

I have been prevailed upon to accept of the office of the fecretary of the Lord Lieutenant of Ireland, in the firm perfuafion and confidence, that his *Majefty's prefent minifters* † are fincere in their profeffions; *and that* THEY *are earneftly difpofed to make fuch conceffions to Ireland, as fhall quiet their jealoufies, and give fatisfaction to their minds.* If I had not had this opinion of the King's Minifters, no circumftance on earth fhould have induced me to take a fituation which at any time I would not have coveted, *and which only fuch opinion and confidence would make me endure.* It is the wife policy of this country, to make thofe conceffions, as from the eftablifhment of a firm and friendly relation, founded upon clear, and known conftitution, *the moft happy confequences will be derived to both countries.*   *April* 9, 1782.

Mr. F O X.

Ireland, may perhaps think of frefh grievances, and rife yearly in her demands; it is fit and proper therefore, that fomething fhould be now done towards eftablifhing on a firm and folid bafis, *the future connexion of the two kingdoms;* but that is to be propofed by me here in parliament; it will be be the duty of the Crown to look to that; *the bu-ſineſs may be firſt begun by his Majeſty's ſervants in Ireland* *; and if afterwards it ſhall be neceſſary to enter into a treaty, commiſſioners may be ſent from the Britiſh parliament, or from the Crown, to enter upon it, and to bring the negociation to a happy iſſue, by giving mutual ſatisfaction to both countries, and eſtabliſhing a treaty, which ſhall be ſanctified by the moſt ſolemn forms of the conſti-tution of both countries.

I have no doubt, but that in affection, as well as in *intereſt*, Ireland and Great Britain will be *but one people*. If any man ſhould entertain any gloomy ideas on the ſubject, let him look at the conclud-ing paragraph of the Iriſh addreſſes; where he will find, that the Iriſh people and parliament *are filled with the moſt earneſt deſires to ſupport England*, to have the ſame enemy and the ſame friend; in a word, *to ſtand or fall with England*. Let gentle-men look forward to that happy period, when Ireland ſhall experience the bleſſings, *that attend freedom of trade and conſtitution*; when by the richneſs and fertility of her ſoil, the induſtry of her manufactures, and the encreaſe of her popu-lation, ſhe ſhall become a powerful country; *then*

D   *may*

* Surely Mr. *Pitt* cannot but be conſidered as extremely for-tunate, in having proceeded in a manner, *ſo ſtrongly recommended by* Mr. FOX.

may England look *for powerful affiftance in feamen to man her fleets, and foldiers to fight her battles.*

England renouncing all right to legiflate for Ireland, the latter will moft cordially fupport the former, as a friend whom fhe loves ; if this country, on the one hand, is to affume the power of making laws for Ireland, fhe will only make an enemy inftead of a friend ; *for where there is a community of intereft*,* and a mutual regard for thofe interefts, there the party whofe interefts are facrificed becomes as enemy.

Upon the whole, I am convinced that the Irifh defire nothing more ardently, *than proper grounds for being moft cordially united to England,* and I am fure that they will be attached to this country *even to bigotry.* *May* 17, 1782.

General BURGOYNE.

I cannot prevail upon myfelf to give a filent vote ; the great revolution that has been affected, with fo much calmnefs and fteadinefs, does the higheft honour to Ireland; and I cannot exprefs myfelf better in praife of the characters who have effected it, upon the greateft principles of freedom, than in the words of the Roman author, *eos qui de nihilo nifi libertate cogitant, dignos effe qui Romani fiant.*

* Such a one as the *prefent* minifter propofes to eftablifh.

fiant. Thofe who know how to think fo juftly of
it, *deferves to be free.* May 17, 1782.

Lord BEUCHAMP.

It is not the mere repeal of the 6 Geo. 1. that
will fatisfy Ireland, becaufe the repeal will leave
the queftion juft as it was before. May 17, 1782.

Mr. BURKE.

It is not on fuch a day as this, when there is
not a difference of opinion *, that I will rife to
fight the battle of Ireland ; *her caufe is neareft my
heart,* and nothing gave me fo much fatisfaction,
when I was firft honoured with a feat in this Houfe,
as it might be in my power, *fome way or other, to
be of fervice to the country that gave me birth †;* and
I have always faid to myfelf, that if fuch an in-
fignificant member as I am, can ever be fo fortu-
nate as to render an effential fervice to England,
and that my fovereign, or parliament, were going
to reward me for it, I would fay to them—*do fomething for Ireland—do fomething for my country, and I
am over-rewarded*——I am a friend to my country,

D 2   but

* Refpecting the repeal of the 6 of Geo. 1.

† There furely then can be but little doubt of the minifter's
having Mr. *Burke's* fupport in carrying his commercial regulations,
between Great Britain and Ireland, through the Houfe.

but gentlemen need not be jealous of that; for in being the friend of Ireland, I deem myſelf of courſe the friend of England—*their intereſts are inſeparable.* *May* 17, 1782.*

Mr. EDEN†.

It was wiſdom in the Iriſh Parliament to chuſe an undefined expreſſion upon a ſubject ſo complicated and extenſive in all its connexions and conſequences; the whole conſideration is now opened to both kingdoms, *and it is the intereſt of both to come to an early kind of efficient concluſion* ‡.

It is a political truth, that happineſs and ſtrength ſhould be extended *through the conſtituent parts of an Empire,* as far as wiſe and beneficial laws can operate to that effect. It would next be eaſy to ſhew, that public happineſs and ſtrength are dif-fuſed in proportion to the plenty and convenience with which not only the natural wants of a people are

* Mr. *Fox* on this day moved, that it is the opinion of this committee (the Houſe being then in a committee) that the intereſts of Great Britain and Ireland *are inſeparable,* and that their connexion *ought to be founded on a ſolid and permanent baſis,* to which the committee agreed without a debate.

† See his letter, entitled, A Letter on the Repreſentations of Ireland, reſpecting a Free Trade.

‡ Page 140.

are fupplied, but fuch adventitious ones as are fuperinduced by univerfal habit and induftry: when this end is not attained to a certain degree, an Empire may indeed exift, and may encreafe in numbers, but it will grow like an unwieldy body, liable to dangers and acute humours *.

Whatever may have been the fyftem of government adopted, or accepted by Ireland, the recent and moft interefting fact is, that fhe now complains of fome diftreffes which fhe conceives to refult from that fyftem. Thefe diftreffes are poffibly no more than have refulted from temporary caufes ;—from the late rebellion with the Colonies, or from the calamities incident to war ; but we know perfectly, that the complaint is founded in real fufferings. The firft inference which would arife from this fact, in any mind reafoning kindly towards a part of the Empire, and difcreetly in refpect of the whole, *is, that the Irifh, as fellow fubjects, are intitled to every relief compatible with the general interefts* †.

If we were to ftate to an Irifh gentleman, the long continued poverty and idlenefs which have prevailed over fo large a proportion of his countrymen, he would probably anfwer——

" All this may be true, but the monopolizing " fpirit of our fifter kingdom is the caufe of it: " that

" that fpirit exercifing itfelf upon Ireland in a
" very early ftate of her civilization, nipped her
" difpofition to induftry, and, inded, made it im-
" poffible for her to become induftrious. In the
" very infancy of our country, and whilft we
" were contenting ourfelves with the exportations
" and fale of our cattle, you made an act * to
" prohibit thofe exportations. We next gave our
" attention to the increafe of our fheep, in order
" to export wool, but you forthwith † prohibited
" the exportation of wool, and made it fubject to
" forfeiture. We then endeavoured to employ
" and fupport ourfelves by falting provifions for
" fale ; but you immediately ‡ refufed them ad-
" mittance into England, in order to encreafe the
" rents of your lands, though you thereby en-
" creafed the wages of your labourers. We next
" began the woollen manufacture ; but it was no
" fooner eftablifhed than deftroyed ; for you pro-
" hibited § the exportation of manufactured wool-
" lens to any other place than England and Wales,
" and this prohibition alone is reported to have
" forced twenty thoufand manufacturers out of the
" kingdom.
" The

---

* 8 Eliz. ch. 3.   † 13 and 14 Car. II. ch. 18.
‡ 18 Car. II. ch. 2.   § 10 and 11 Will. III: ch. 10.

" The Navigation Act ‖ had unwittingly, but
" kindly, permitted all commodities to be im-
" ported into Ireland, upon the same terms as in-
" to England: but by an act * passed three years
" afterwards, the exportation of any goods from
" Ireland into any of the plantations was prohi-
" bited: and as if that had not sufficiently crippled
" the benefits given by the Navigation Act, we
" were soon † afterwards forbid to import any of
" the enumerated commodities from the plantations
" into Ireland. This restriction too was much
" enforced by subsequent acts, and the list of
" enumerated goods was much encreased. I say
" nothing of your regulations respecting glass,
" hops, sail-cloth, &c. ‡ and other inferior barriers
" and obstructions to our commerce: we subsisted
" under all this, and under a drain also, which
" has gradually encreased upon us, by remittances
" to our own absentees, English mortgages, Go-
" vernment annuitants, and other extra-commer-
" cial purposes, to the amount of half a million
" sterling annually. And though we retained no
" trade but in linen, and provisions, the latter has
" been under a three years prohibition, during
" which period we lost the principal market for
" our own beef, though three-fourths of our peo-
" ple

‖ 12 Car. II. ch. 10.   * 10 and 11 Will. III. ch. 10.
† 22 Car. II. ch. 18.   ‡ 15 Car. II. ch. 7.

" ple were graziers. Many of us, indeed, carried
" on a clandeſtine trade, and it was eſſential to
" our ſupport; but that too has been lately check-
" ed firſt by the revolt of the colonies, and now
" by the war with France and Spain.

" Our annual remittances and debts to Great-
" Britain now encreaſe with our diſtreſſes: our
" ſubſcriptions for loans have been lately filled
" from Great-Britain; our eſtates, when ſold, are
" purchaſed by Engliſhmen; our leaſes, when
" they expire, are raiſed by abſentees; the drain
" is become greater than all our means can ſup-
" ply; our manufacturers find little demand for
" their work; the farmers ſell their produce with
" difficulty; our land rents, indeed, are eſtimated
" at near three millions ſterling, but our land-
" holders will ſoon be obliged to reduce them.
" We allow that ſeveral of your reſtrictions upon
" us, have lately been much ſoftened, or modified,
" but the want of an annual profit in our inter-
" courſe with Great-Britain equal to our remittan-
" ces ſtill prevails, and is every hour more felt.
" By the unfortunate ſituation of the colonies, we
" have loſt even our old refuge in emigrations.
" After having for many years taken Britiſh ma-
" nufactures, to the annual amount of *two millions*
" ſterling, we are for the preſent reduced to *non-*
" *importation*

" *importation* agreements *, as a meafure, not of
" expediency, but of neceffity. It would have
" fuited the generofity of our feelings, and the
" affection which we bear towards you, to have
" made our reprefentations in better and more
" peaceable times; but you fee that our circum-
" ftances are urgent, *and that your recent indul-*
" *gences are infufficient. We defire, therefore* A FREE
" TRADE, *otherwife our diftreffes muft, if poffible,*
" *encreafe, and the conveniency of our ports will con-*
" *tinue of no more ufe to us, than a beautiful profpect*
" *to a man fhut up in a dungeon†.*"

Great-Britain *lofes whenever Ireland is deprived of*
any reafonable gain—and with refpect to the fituation of the latter for the weftern navigation, we
know that it is the intereft of a dominion to carry
on her commerce, from whatever corner fhe can
conduct it to the beft advantage, and it would be
thought a grofs abfurdity in the city of London,
if becaufe Briftol is fo fituated as to have an ad-

E   vantage

* It ought to have been anfwered, " We *(the Irifh)* fend
" more than that to England, with this difference, that the
" whole amount of ours, is the produce, or manufacture of
" Ireland——the true fource of the wealth of a country;
" while the half of Englifh exports are of foreign produce.—-
" Non-importation would have raifed in Ireland—we take more
" than 1,000,000l. of their linens, and they take 3,000,000l.
" of our woollens—the two ftaples."

† Page 146.

vantage in the Irifh trade, *the former fhould defire
to have the port of the latter fhut up.*

In all thefe reafonings, the commercial and political interefts, *are infeparably blended.* When the
liberty of commerce *is unequally enjoyed*, one part of
an empire may be in danger of becoming a burden
to the other. An increafe of fupport in and of
the common exertions, might, in courfe of time,
refult to Ireland from the advancement of her
trade, and from the produce of duties, analogous
to thofe of Great-Britain.

It is fometimes found, that a liberty to export
manufactures, increafes the produce of raw materials beyond the demand of the particular manufacture; and from the experience of the linen
trade, it might be doubted whether lefs woollen
yarn would be exported to Great-Britain by Ireland, if the export of manufactured woollens were
lefs reftrained; in which cafe, the fmuggling of
raw wool to the Continent of Europe might be
checked*.

We are not, however, to proceed with that
fhort-fighted wifdom, which may enable us to fhun
the mere difficulty of a day; nor to act upon the
fpur of a moment †.

The Irifh, though at all times, fhe has had full
liberty to manufacture goods for her own confumption,

[27]

tion, the confumers have hitherto found it eafier to purchafe from England many articles, both of luxury and convenience, than to make them at home. Amidft the difficulties which time, and the foftering attention of this country, alone can enable Ireland to overcome, it deferves remark, that fhe has little coal, is ill provided with wood, and is nearly without inland navigations. In fhort, the conftitution and eftablifhment of a flourifhing empire, imply a well regulated order throughout the nation, a fteady and effective police, habits of docility and induftry, fkill in manufactures, and large capitals in trade; all which can be the refult only of a continued and gradual progrefs, aided by a combination of other favouring circumftances *.

Colonel FITZPATRICK †.

I am anxious that fatisfaction fhould be given to the Irifh nation, and that they fhould learn that this country is well difpofed *to give every neceffary fatisfaction.* This is particularly to be wifhed, becaufe pains have been taken to fpread ideas, that what has been done is not fufficient for the fecurity of Ireland, and furmifes have been thrown out

E 2   againft

* Page 166.

† Colonel Fitzpatrick begged leave to call the attention of Government to the circumftance, which had given fome blame to the people of Ireland, *the decifion of an Irifh caufe in the Court of King's Bench in England.*

againſt the friends of order and reaſon, *who were convinced of the rectitude of the intentions of Britain.*

Dec. 19, 1782.

Mr. F O X.

I take the firſt moment to declare, that the intentions of thoſe Miniſters who ſent the repeal of the Declaratory Act, *were thereby to make a complete, abſolute, and perpetual ſurrender of the Britiſh legiſlature and judicial ſupremacy over Ireland.* THIS *was the intention of Government* *; and it is clear to the conviction, both of Miniſters and of the Gentlemen of Ireland, who intereſted themſelves in the buſineſs, that the manner in which this is done, is the beſt poſſible way, and the leaſt liable to exception.

Dec. 19, 1782.

Lord B E A U C H A M P.

I have always underſtood it to be the privilege of a Member of Parliament, that when he has any particular buſineſs in the Houſe, it was not to be taken out of his hands *by another* †. This is a privilege I would never reſign ; a friend to *both* kingdoms,

---

* No one will ſurely diſpute Mr. *Fox's* authority.

† This was occaſioned by Mr. *William Grenville* giving notice, that he ſhould move for a call of the Houſe, *at an earlier day* than the 22'd of January (the day on which Lord Beauchamp moved the Call) when a motion would be made relative to Ireland.

kingdoms, my only object is to fecure *a lafting har-mony* betwen Great Britain and Ireland; and if I fhould be able to root out every remains of jea-loufy, *my* great object will be accomplifhed, and I fhall fit down *the happieft of men !*

Mr. E D E N.

A diffatisfaction has fomehow fince arifen, but I ftill continue to think, that it ought not to have arifen, for it fhewed beyond a poffible doubt*, not merely the good faith, but the induftrious anxi-ety of England, *to gratify Ireland in the point of free legiflation.*

I feel myfelf ever difpofed to think, and to fpeak of Ireland with gratitude, with affection, and with refpect ; but I do not think her at this hour an ob-ject of fear to any nation under the Sun ; fhe neither has, nor will have her due importance in the great fcale of the globe, till fhe can be induced to think herfelf fecure *in quitting politics, and purfuing com-merce ; it is my object and wifh to forward for her that happy and important moment.*   *Jan.* 22, 1783.

Mr. F O X.

By the actual repeal of the 6 Geo. I. Great Britain certainly, *and to all intents and purpofes,* re-linquifhed *every fhadow of jurifdiction, and fupremacy.*
                                   Jan. 22, 1783.

---

* Mr. Fox's propofition on the 17th of May.

Mr. EDEN.

I relied on a treaty being opened † between the Parliaments of Great Britain and Ireland, for the purpofes of arranging not only the points already fpecified, but all the great queftions involved in the future events of peace and war, foreign alliances, commercial treaties, limitation of armies, building and fupport of navies. Proportionable fupplies, *with the whole immenfe detail under each of thofe heads.* I fhall then, *and not till then,* think that the connection is eftablifhed; and when the two kingdoms have thus realized and fecured one conftitution, one commerce, one King, one friend, one enemy, and one fate, it will become impoffible for any man, *to wifh the profperity of the one country more ardently, or more earneftly, than the profperity of the other.*

Jan. 22, 1783.

† When I voted for the addrefs of the 17th of May laft.

HOUSE of LORDS.

Earl of HILLSBOROUGH.

I WAS called by my Sovereign, from a private fituation, to affift in his councils. I had formed my opinion, as an object of leading confequence, refpecting the ftate of Ireland. I imparted my thoughts, my motives, and intended conduct, to thofe with whom I am to act; *and upon the idea of a full confirmation, and fupport of the Crown and its fervants, I confented to come into office.*

I wifh not to be underftood, as dictating any meafures, or pledging myfelf for the refult; what I mean is merely this, that fuch and fuch were my opinions; that they were approved of, and that I would wait with anxious fufpence, and chearfully abide the event, and in common with the reft of his Majefty's fubjects, fubmit to the fenfe of Parliament; but if, on the other hand, as fuggefted as a general charge againft Government, that the conditions on which I came into place, fhould be

violated,

violated, or departed from, or that a perfect good faith should not be preserved, the same motives which induced me to accept of the seals, a view to serve my country, *to cause relief to be given to Ireland,* and advance the interest and prosperity of every part of the British Empire, would point out to me the propriety of retiring again into a private station; *when the end for which I left it ★,* shall be found no longer attainable, or in other words, *when it will not be in my power to secure my country.*   *Nov.* 25, 1779 †.

Earl

★ To procure, in conjunction with the rest of the Ministers of the Crown, such relief for Ireland, as she might be entitled to expect from Great Britain.

† On the 11th May, 1779, the *late Marquis of Rockingham* moved an immediate consideration of the distressed, and impoverished state of the kingdom of Ireland, and such effectual measures as should promote *the common strength, wealth, and commerce of his Majesty's subjects in Great Britain and Ireland.*—After describing the *private* as well as *public* distresses of Ireland, in the most feeling language, the noble Marquis proceeded to contrast the deserts of the Irish nation, whose loyalty kept pace with the extent and magnitude of the calamities they felt. He instanced, in particular, their friendly and affectionate behaviour since the commencement of the American war; the zeal and fidelity of that kingdom, in the time of the two last Scotch rebellions; the uncommon efforts she made during the late war, and her uniform loyalty, and attachment, to this country, in every trying exigency, when engaged in a foreign war.

He

He faid, he hoped, the importance of the fubject would ftrike every noble Lord with the propriety, nay, the abfolute neceffity of his motion, that the Houfe would treat it *with that temper' coolnefs, and moderation* which it fo apparently merited, and attend to' it as a matter, in which every man in the nation was moft deeply interefted. He trufted, that their Lordfhips would not be led away *by any partial ideas or narrow diftinctions of local benefit or advantage* *, but meet it fairly as a queftion of State, in which both kingdoms had an equal intereft. He would be extremely forry, this, or that town, or diftrict, *that Manchefter, or Glafgow, or any other place, would fupercede or render of non-effect the wifdom of their Lordfhips' deliberations.* He wifhed farther, that on the prefent occafion, *all party or perfonal confiderations would give way to the general good* †, and that as they all meant *the fame thing,* the interefts of both kingdoms, their Lordfhips' would not entertain a fecond opinion on the fubject. It was a great object, and fhould neither be loft, abandoned, or evaded; it had for fome years been unfortunately too much neglected, but matters were at length arrived juft at that critical ftate, which would render it not only unwife and impolitic to lofe a moment, but would afford an inftance of obftinacy and want of feeling, *little fhort of political infanity.*

* The noble Marquis appears to be well aware *of the partial ideas, and narrow diftinctions, of local benefit, or advantage,* that would probably *be ftirred up againft* the adjufting fuch a commercial intercourfe, as might be thought for the *reciprocal* benefit of both countries; and no doubt, the Houfe of Lords will be fufficiently guarded againft any thing of the kind, on the prefent occafion.

† It is to be hoped that Mr. Fox, and his friends, will bear in mind the falutary advice and wholefome admonition of the noble Marquis, whofe virtues they fo juftly revered, and whofe memory they hold fo dear, and not fuffer the real intereft of Great-Britain and Ireland to give way *to party or perfonal confiderations.*

F   Earl

Earl of HILSBOROUGH.

Previous to my acceptance of the feals, as Secretary of State, I defired to know the intention of his Majefty's Minifters *(Lord North, &c.)* and the opinion of his Council, relative to future meafures, refpecting Ireland; and received every affurance from them, that Government was thoroughly difpofed to co-operate with Parliament, in giving to that kingdom, *fuch an extenfion of trade as would put her on a footing with Great-Britain on the fcale of commerce* *. *Dec.* 1, 1779 ‡.

---

* As the *memory* of Lord North, and his friends, are fo apt to fail them, it is rather a *lucky* circumftance for them, that it can be refrefhed by fo refpectable an authority.

‡ The late Marquis of Rockingham was fo very fenfible of the neceffity there was for doing fomething for effectually relieving the diftreffes of Ireland, and had the object fo much at heart, that in the courfe of the debate on the 11th of May, 1779, he repeated with fome warmth, that Ireland had been cruelly and injurioufly treated, and that it would prefent a mixture of folly and ingratitude, which nothing but the dulleft obftinacy and ignorance could explain, if we refufe to lighten *thofe intolerable burthens* which the reftriction *of our trade laws* laid upon that *loyal, affectionate, and enduring people.* The *Duke of Beaufort,* though he poffeffed a confiderable property in Ireland, faid he fhould chearfully affift in any meafure, for giving the Irifh that fpecies of relief which their fituation demanded. *Lord Townfhend,* in expreffions of the warmeft affections for the people of Ireland, pleaded

Earl GOWER.

I had the good fortune to unite the Houfe laft Seffion, upon the terms of the Addrefs to the Throne *. I was in hopes that fomething *effectual*

F 2   for

pleaded their diftreffes and deferts in very forcible language ; and faid, he fhould be wanting in the feelings which gratitude ough^t ever to infpire, if he did not take the prefent opportunity of teftifying his regard for them, and his earneftnefs to procure them every degree of redrefs and indulgence, which their melancholy fituation demanded, which juftice dictated, and generofity and national gratitude rendered a pofitive duty on the part of a great nation. He fhould, in point of union and national ftrength, *ever confider England and Ireland as one country, and the people of each equally bound and connected by the fame object, the profperity of the whole.* The *Duke of Richmond* alfo in a very able fpeech, endeavoured to fhow, that all local diftinction were the creatures of prejudice and felfifhnefs. He faid, that Ireland and England *were in fact the fame nation and people* ; that any diftinction made in favour of the *latter*, was a piece of injuftice to the *former*. A great, loyal, and a brave people, were not to be ruined, beggared, or oppreffed, becaufe Manchefter thought *this*, or *this*, or *that country were alarmed.* All thefe petty motives muft ceafe to operate, nor be permitted to influence our public Councils, which ought never to lofe fight of juftice and found policy. He was for an union; but not an union of Legiflature, *but an union of hearts, hands, of affections, and interefts.*

* The Addrefs was as follows :—" That this Houfe take into " confideration the diftreffed and impoverifhed ftate of the kingdom " of Ireland, and being of opinion, that it is confonant to juftice

" and

for the relief of Ireland would have arifen *from the unanimous concurrence of their Lordſhips* in the amendment I then had the honour to propoſe †. If however, nothing has been done, for the relief of that country, which I am pretty ſure is the caſe, I aſſure the Houſe, that I have done every thing in my power to keep my word, which I formerly pledged to the Houſe, and am ready to acknowledge,

" and true policy to remove the cauſes of diſcontent by a redreſs
" of grievances, and, in order to demonſtrate the ſenſe which the
" Houſe entertains of the merits of that loyal and well deſerving
" nation, this Houſe doth think it highly expedient, that this im-
" portant buſineſs ſhould be no longer neglected, and that an hum-
" ble Addreſs be preſented to his Majeſty, That his Majeſty would
" be graciouſly pleaſed to take the matter into his moſt ſerious
" conſideration, and direct his Miniſter to prepare, and lay before
" Parliament ſuch particulars relative to the trade and manufac-
" tures of Ireland, as may enable the national wiſdom to purſue
" effectual meaſures for promoting the common ſtrength, wealth,
" and commerce, of his Majeſty's ſubjects in both kingdoms."

† The following is the *amended* addreſs which was carried *nem. con.* " That an humble addreſs be preſented to his Majeſty, that
" he will be pleaſed to take into his gracious conſideration, the
" diſtreſſed and impoveriſhed ſtate of the loyal and well-deſerving
" people of Ireland, and to direct an account to be laid before
" Parliament of ſuch particulars relative to the trade and manu-
" factures of Ireland, as may enable the national wiſdom to pur-
" ſue methods for promoting the common ſtrength, wealth, and
" commerce, of his Majeſty's ſubjects in both kingdoms."

knowledge, but I muſt add, in my own juſtificati-
on, that my efforts have proved totally unfruitful.

May 11, 1779*.

Earl of CARLISLE.

I riſe to expreſs my entire approbation of the
motion †, and to bear my teſtimony to the zeal

* His Lordſhip added, that he had, for ſome years, preſided at
the Council Table, and had ſeen ſuch things paſs there, that no
man of honour and conſcience, could any longer ſit there. The
ſituation of Great Britain and Ireland required *ſincerity and acti-
vity of Council.* There is no doubt as to the cauſe of the noble Earl's
diſguſt.—The miniſters (*Lord North,* &c.) had certainly pledged
themſelves to do ſomething *effectual for the Relief of Ireland,* and
none was given.

† " Firſt, That it is the opinion of this Houſe, that the Act of
" 6th Geo. I. intitled, an Act for the better ſecuring the depen-
" dency of Ireland upon the Crown of Great Britain, ought to
" be repealed. Second, That it is the opinion of this Houſe,
" That it is indiſpenſible to the intereſt and happineſs of both
" countries, that the connection between them ſhould be eſtabliſh-
" ed by mutual conſent, upon a ſolid and permanent footing, and
" that an humble addreſs be preſented to his Majeſty, that his
" Majeſty will be graciouſly pleaſed, to take ſuch meaſures as his
" Majeſty in his royal wiſdom ſhall think moſt conducive to that
" important end." Both motions were agreed to without a diviſion. Both the Reſolutions were moved by the Earl of Shelburne,
and ſupported by the Earl of Carliſle, Lord Camden, Duke of
Leinſter, Duke of Chandos, and Duke of Richmond.

and

and loyalty of the Irish, particularly of the honourable conduct of the Volunteers, and the liberal offers made of their service, when Ireland was threatened with an attack. Had I been more persuaded than I am, that Ireland had ever relinquished its right of free legislation, which I know they neither have nor can give up, I should still have thought it wise to accede to their claim; because I know, that from the gratitude and affection of the country, and the wisdom of Parliament, much more advantage would arise to Great Britain, than by maintaining any offensive and ill-founded pretensions to a controul over them.

May 17, 1782.

Earl of HILSBOROUGH.

I hope, and believe, ministers are sincere in their good intentions towards Ireland. I am persuaded, they have no other object with regard to this country, and to that, but to promote the interest of both; but persons at a distance, *who are not so well convinced of their good intention towards Ireland**, may construe every little delay into matter

---

* It is now three years since the noble Lord was promised by *Lord North, &c.* that relief should be given to Ireland, and though none has ever been rendered, yet the noble Lord has still so much faith in their assurances, *as to believe them sincere in their intentions towards*

matter of fufpicion and alarm; and, therefore, I conceive, *I beſt ſhow myſelf the friend of Government, by cautioning them of their danger.*

June 3, 1783.

Duke of PORTLAND.

I always have been, and always ſhall be ready, to do every thing in my power to cement the connection between Great Britain and Ireland, on terms of mutual affection and mutual intereſt.

April 24, 1783.†

towards Ireland, nay, for his Lordſhip's part, *he is perſuaded of it,* whatever perſons may think, *who are at a diſtance,* and may conſtrue every little delay *into matter of fuſpicion and alarm.*—What will the noble Lord think then, ſhould this ſame *Lord North* be found to oppoſe the commercial intercourſe now eſtabliſhing between Great Britain and Ireland?

† On the ſecond reading of the Iriſh Judicature Bill.

APPENDIX.

THE

COMMERCIAL RESOLUTIONS

OF THE

IRISH PARLIAMENT,

IN THEIR PRESENT SESSION,

VINDICATED.

Abstract of a Letter from a Member of the British House of Commons, written soon after the late General Election, to a Member of the Irish House.

SIR,   *May*, 1784.

WHEN Ireland was dependent on Great Britain, it was wished by several friends of both Countries to render dependence beneficial to her. Two bills were therefore brought into the British Parliament, one allowing to Ireland freedom of Exportation to our Colonies and Settlements, the other a like Freedom of Importation from thence, both denied to all Foreign Independent countries.

G   These

Thefe were meant as experiments, upon a narrow fcale, which, if found advantageous to Ireland without prejudicing Britain, might and ought to be extended further ; were it for no other purpofe than to preferve Irifh dependence by the fureft and only juftifiable means.

The firft Bill paffed, but abfurdly mutilated; and the little that remained of it was rendered ufelefs by a ftill more abfurd fuppreffion of the fecond Bill, as an export-trade cannot fubfift where imports are prohibited.

When Ireland became independent, with an unreftrained freedom of trade to all countries except Great Britain, I wifhed her friendfhip fhould be preferved by opening the Ports of Great Britain upon the fame terms that open thofe of Ireland to Her, convinced as I then was and ftill am that the comparative magnitude of Britifh Capitals, lownefs of intereft and fuperiority of fkill, with all their neceffary confequences, would, under an equality of duties, fecure a continuance of the fame advantages to Great Britain which fhe before invidioufly poffeffed under an inequality which operated as a total Prohibition on her fide of almoft all manufactures except Linen, while fhe was treated in Ireland *literally*, as the moft favoured Nation in the fcale of duties.

I am aware of the objection, that when Ireland becomes rich, thofe advantages will leffen with her increafe and at length totally ceafe. But wealth, earned and employed in trade, will ever in a progreffive ftate maintain at leaft the fuperiority it had gained : improvements of old manufactures and difcoveries of new will more frequently appear, as they now do at Manchefter, Birmingham, &c. &c. and Dublin growing *richer* in her progreffive ftate, but advancing by flower paces, will become a better cuftomer than *poor* Dublin ever was.

But, be this as it may, independent Ireland will never be fatiffied under the prefent inequality of duties. It is a badge of flavery which fhe never will patiently bear, and the Britifh Parliament alone has the means of removing it, by lowering the duties there to the Irifh ftandard. The attempt now meditating in Ireland to increafe them there in the article of woollens, fupported by the moft falfe affertions and moft abfurd arguments, would, if it could fucceed, certainly be fatal to Ireland, as it would foon be retaliated by England on linens and other articles, while multiplied reftraints would at length end in a total prohibition of trade in both countries, fuch as is only known in a ftate of war; yet England even now is the beft cuftomer Ireland has, giving a
                                                                    longer

longer credit than any other country can for what she sends, and paying quicker remittances for what she receives : Two returns in a year upon the same capital, which double its profits, make one thoufand pounds virtually as much as two, where returns are made but once in the fame fpace of time.

You have here the thoughts of an old infirm man, who has bid farewell to all politics, Englifh and Irifh : and who, though elected into this Parliament, is determined to vacate his feat; yet, if you think as I do upon this fubject, and believe that the expedient will fatisfy Ireland, I will defer the execution of my unalterable purpofe, until I fhall have had an early opportunity of throwing myfelf and my opinions upon the Houfe of Commons, as I have often done without hazard to the popularity of Minifters, with whom I was connected, if my opinion were not relifhed; and willing to give them all the merit if they were approved. In this fpirit I now write to you and have the honour to be, &c. &c.

PURPORT OF THE ANSWER

RECEIVED TO THE

ABOVE LETTER.

" NOTHING but protecting duties, heavier upon Merchan-
" dife imported from Great Britain than upon Irifh Merchandife
" imported there, will fatisfy Ireland."

WHILE a fyftem of duties feemed to be thus infifted upon by Ireland, not equalized by the value of fimilar aaticles in commerce, as is the univerfal rule of Tariffs between all Independent States : while in that fyftem allowances were claimed for the infe-

rior abilities of Ireland to fupply Great Britain to purchafe from
her the fame articles at the fame rates, impoffible to be propor-
tioned fo as to form a fair ftandard of Trade ; and while thefe
arbitrary conditions were to be impofed by threats and violence
proceeding to avert acts of cruel Barbarifin, no friend of both
countries would infult Great Britain by offering propofitions to
her Parliament, which if accepted there, would be reprobated and
fpurned by the Irifh Parliament, the whole Nation applauding
their conduct.

Thus circumftanced I retire in defpair, and if the Minifters of
Great Britain had then introduced any accommodating propofitions here, in the firft inftance, they, inftead of afferting the dignity
of their country by infifting upon that precedence, would have
tarnifhed and debafed it : Thofe who are in the wrong fhould firft
make conceffions ; or if, as happily was the fact in Ireland, fac-
tion, ignorance and frenzy, did not fpeak the fentiments of the
people, it behoved the honour and fidelity of their reprefentatives
to declare the difference, by offering a plan to the fifter Kingdom
fupported, and only fupported by Equality, Juftice and mutual
Intereft.

But if, having thus acted, the Britifh Parliament fhould again
be influenced, as it was in the two Bills already mentioned, by
the miftaken intereft of narrow-minded men againft one common
univerfal intereft the Irifh Parliament, though without a profpect
of Ireland ever becoming the Emporium of trade, as was hyper-
bolically expreffed in a late debate, would be the unrivall'd pof-
feffor of firmnefs, liberality, reafon and juftice.

Vilius argentum eft auro, virtutibus aurum.

That an oppofition here to the Refolutions of the Irifh Parliament proceeds from falfe conceptions, we fhall now endeavour to
prove by ftating thofe objections which have reached our knowledge ; and giving the anfwers which have occurred to us.

OBJECTION I. If Ireland be permitted to export Sugars to
Great Britain, fhe will fmuggle in for that purpofe Foreign Sugars
purchafed at a lower price ; and by thefe means underfel Britifh
Sugars at their own home market.

ANSWER. The Revenue of Ireland would then fuffer doubly.
Firft, by being defrauded of the duty payable upon imported
Mufcavado Sugars, and again by paying upon their exportation
a draw-

a drawback of duties never received, or a premium when refined, more than an equivalent for thofe duties. The Parliament and Government of Ireland will therefore be moft importantly interefted in preventing that practice.

Secondly, The Irifh confumption of Sugars is confiderable, and is chiefly, if not intirely, of Sugars brought from Great Britain. Why then is not that confumption now entirely fupplied with fmuggled Sugars? thefe would find a demand to a confiderable amount, although the Britifh Ports were, as they ftill are, fhut to Irifh exportation.

OBJECTION II. French, Dutch, Danifh, &c. Sugars, will be entered as our Plantation Sugars, and, though they pay the fame duties, they will be bought cheaper, and fo circumftanced will be exported to Britain entitled to a drawback there of the duties paid, or to a premium, as the cafe fhall happen upon re-exportation.

ANSWER. The Irifh Revenue will be no gainer by this traffic, and therefore the Government will have no intereft in conniving at it. Nor is the difference of price fuch as to tempt the fraudulent Merchant to encounter the rifk of being difcovered.

OBJECTION III. Irifh Merchants would be the fole importers of Sugars into Ireland directly from the Britifh Plantations.

ANSWER. This objection is the reverfe of the foregoing, but the fecond anfwer is applicable to it : The Irifh are at liberty now to import Sugars directly, to the full amount of Irifh confumption, yet fmall have been the quantities fo imported, fince the freedom of a direct importation has been allowed to Ireland.

OBJECTION IV. Britifh Merchants will tranfport themfelves and their capitals into Ireland.

ANSWER. Why is not this fuppofition verified by fome inftances now to be produced? They certainly will not fend their capitals, and ftay themfelves behind, trufting to the management of others. But inconvenient and difagreeable as this removal would be to themfelves and their families, they would find it more difficult to procure fugar-bakers to remove, and perfuade all the fubordinate manufactures to accompany them. Yet fhould this be effected, they cannot tranfport their fugar-houfes, nor the materials of which they are built. They muft be fold here at the price of rubbifh; for the buildings cannot be converted to new ufes;

and

and the fame is true of the utenfils. All thefe muft again be provided in Ireland, when the adventurers arrive there, where it
will be found, that coals, and many other articles neceffary to
the refining of Sugars, are dearer than in England.

But thefe are far from being all the difadvantages to be encoun-
tered in Ireland : a credit of three years, ufually given to the
planter by the merchant his creditor, muft ftill be continued,
while the fugar-baker and refiner will require from the merchant
a longer refpite of payment than is allowed in England, where
the fhop-keeper, their cuftomer, is fooner and more punctually
paid by the cuftomer. Quick returns of fmall profits, the life of
trade, are only to be found in wealthy countries ; and men fo
enriched, will hardly emigrate into poor countries, to meet with
delay and difappointments, not to be compenfated by cheapnefs
of manual labour, or commodioufnefs of fituation.

But though mere manual labour, fuch as is employed in delv-
ing and ditching, which require no fkill, may be hired cheaper
from a wretch in poverty and rags, it is much dearer and lefs
valuable in every work of art, fhortened in numberlefs inftances
by engines enabling one man to do more than many. A few years
fince, there was not a fingle crane on the Quay of Cork.

The hiftory of commerce rarely produces an inftance of a
wealthy trader going into a poor country to increafe his wealth :
but if cheapnefs of manual labour neceffarily invited large capitals, no poor country would long continue poor ; nor indeed any
rich country long continue rich, mutually changing and re-chang-
ing conditions, as the price of fuch labour funk or rofe. But
though poverty emigrates, or ftarves, wealth remains fixt to that
foil where it grew ; and flourifhes in proportion as it fpreads its
roots deeper and wider there.——Tranfplant an oak and it pe-
rifhes *.

What has been faid of cheap labour, is equally true of com-
modious fituation. The richeft mercantile towns in England
have the worft harbours : Milford fcarcely contains a veffel in its
excellent haven, except paffing to or from fome other port, while

---

* England underfells Ireland at her own Markets with Cloth made of Irifh
Woollen Yarn, for which a duty is paid in Ireland upon exportation ; and
the difference of price is greater in proportion to the finenefs of the Fabrick.

the dry mud of Briftol is crouded with fhips detained there by many contrary winds, and expofed to fire from the houfes but a few yards diftant, after having made their way through a moft perilous channel to the merchants's warehoufes. Were thofe merchants afked, why they do not remove to Milford Haven? and were the fame queftion propofed to fugar-bakers, glafs-men, copper manufacturers, &c. &c. &c. their anfwer would be, a fmile of contempt. Yet predictions much more impoffible of emigrations to Dublin, Cork, Waterford, and Limerick, are gravely made, and anxioufly liftened to.

But if all we have faid were falfe, and Cork were to rival Briftol, while London would be rivalled by Dublin in Weft Indian imports, though the Britifh merchant would then have a juft caufe for forrow and oppofition, the Weft India planters fhould rejoice in a view of two markets inftead of being confined to one.

This leads us to another objection.

Objection V. The Planter indebted to his factor in Britain, as moft Planters confeffedly are, would change hands and defraud his creditor by confignments into Ireland.

Answer. This expedient though troublefome and expenfive to the Creditor, would not leave him without a remedy, as the Planter's property in the Weft Indies would be fubject to his demand. It is reported that one or two attempts of this nature were made in England, but defeated.

Nor has it, I believe, been heard that fuch bafe policy was, in any inftance, practifed in fupplying the confumption of Ireland ever fince a direct importation has been allowed there.

The planters therefore need not be folicitous to refute fo undeferved a calumny, by uniting with the Britifh Merchants. Nor is fuch folicitude the real caufe of an union clearly accounted for without admitting an infamous imputation upon any number of worthy, but generous men : moft Planters are indebted to their Factors, and by confequence are under their power and influence.

There are however many planters in opulent circumftances, free from all reftraint, who, though the advertifing merchants would blend them in one general defcription, will, no doubt, feparate and diftinguifh themfelves from their enthralled brethren.

But,

But, if what we have advanced upon this subject be well
founded, the merchant requires no sacrifice from the planters of
their interest to his; his fears are as vain as those of a North
British member of Parliament were, when he foretold in a speech
against the importation of Irish live cattle into Britain, that, if
it was permitted, an Ox would be as rare an animal in our fields
as a Lion.

OBJECTION VI. When the ports of Great Britain shall be
always open to the importation of grain and flour from Ireland,
let the price be ever so low; immense quantities will be poured
in from thence, detrimental to the British landlord and tenant.

ANSWER. The dry climate of South Britain is universally
more favourable to harvests, than that of rainy Ireland, and the
same is true of most parts of North Britain. Potatoes are therefore the general food of Ireland. Yet a great proportion of the
comparatively small quantity of grain and flour, consumed there,
was supplied by England, until a bounty was granted in Ireland
upon exportation; and we believe that the balance, though not
so great, is still in favour of England.

Should there be, in an unusual change of seasons, a scarcity
here when there is an abundance in Ireland, a supply from thence
will be more to our advantage, than from any other country,
and Irish cheapness will then be a common blessing to the sister
kingdoms.

But should there be a superfluity in both, Britain will preferably
consume her own grain and flour free from freight and hazard,
which she must pay for; nor will Ireland send her produce to an
over-stocked market, while the World is open to her.

It is true that Scotland, in particular, is supplied with Irish
oats and meal, in great quantities for her own consumption. But
it is also true that Scotch Merchants, and others in parts of South
Britain, purchase more than is wanted for that purpose, immediately after harvest, when the miserable Irish tenant is obliged
to thresh out his corn, for payment of rent in November to a
distressed and relentless landlord. From hence it often happens
that Irish corn is exported at a much lower price, sometimes
scarcely exceeding one half of what it afterwards bears, when
brought back to drained and starving Ireland.

But admitting that North Britain, chiefly concerned in this
question, should sometimes so abound with oats of her own
growth,

growth, as to render a prohibition of importation advantageous, which feldom happens even for a fhort time, fhe will at all other times be a gainer, by cheapnefs in Ireland.

Having vindicated, we hope, fufficiently the Refolutions of the Irifh Parliament, we fhall now take notice of an *objection* made by fome of its members *to the* 10*th Article,* charged with granting a *tribute* annually payable to Britain, as if a fmall contribution to the fupport of a Maritime Force, neceffary to the common protection of both countries, deferved a degrading appellation; more efpecially as the application of that fupply to any fpecifick naval fervice, is to be folely directed by the Irifh Parliament, although it is to arife out of an hereditary revenue, fettled more than a century paft by an Irifh Parliament upon the King of England and Ireland.

The eventual fupply, for fuch it only is, now to be granted, will depend for its exiftence and quantity upon an increafe of Irifh trade, neceffarily requiring a larger eftablifhment of force and expence. If there be no increafe, there will be no fupply, and if there be an increafe, the fupply will rife only in proportion to it.

When affiftance has been purchafed by Great Britain, as it has been almoft in every war, from allies unconnected with her by any common intereft, and without any of the qualifying circumftances, which attend what thofe, whom we have alluded to, call a tribute, however thofe fubfidifed powers may have been blamed for fubmitting to fuch terms, Great Britain has been often ferved but never difhonoured by becoming thus tributary to many a petty Prince. Yet in this fenfe only would Ireland be tributary to Great Britain, for her affiftance by paying an annual fum, more properly termed a fubfidy, than a tribute.

Should the adjuftment now propofed by the Parliament of Ireland be rejected here, God grant that without any degree of prefcience exceeding what is derived from experience and a flight knowledge of Hiftory, we fhall not be better warranted than the abovementioned North Britifh Member was in his prediction, when we foretel that the King of Great Britain and Ireland, while he retains both characters, giving his affent to the bills of each Parliament, will not be able to exercife that function of Royal legiflative power confiftently with the duty of a common Father to all his fubjects.

H

We

We fhall therefore conclude by hoping that whatever oppofition may be confiftently given by thofe who either voted againft
the two bills mentioned in the foregoing abftract, or did not vote
at all, none who joined in their fupport upon the principle that
Great Britain and Ireland fhould retain all their refpective natural or acquired advantages, but fubject to the fame duties upon
importation and upon exportation to Foreign Markets, will op-
pofe a further enlargement of the trade of Ireland grounded upon
the fame principles, certain as it is that the acquired advantages
of Great Britain incomparably exceed the fuperiority of thofe
natural to Ireland. Nay we are far from conceding any fuperiority to Ireland in the fum total of gifts gratuitoufly beftowed
by Providence without Labour and Induftry.

F I N I S.

www.ingramcontent.com/pod-product-compliance
Lightning Source LLC
Chambersburg PA
CBHW031757090426
42739CB00008B/1043